THE ENDANGERED SPECIES
ELEPHANTS

BY TARA MOORE

Garrard Publishing Company

Champaign, Illinois
Easton, Maryland

PUBLISHER'S NOTE

Her name is Tara Moore. She is an American artist—a photographer and a painter who has spent a great deal of time painting members of the wild kingdom. Tara has traveled widely in pursuit of her love for these animals—from the sweltering bush country of Africa to the steamy jungles of Asia; to the frozen wasteland of the Arctic regions. She seeks to bring to young readers a real appreciation of wild animals, their fascinating habitats, their needs, and their timeless ways of life. Her aim is to teach the young reader a crucial lesson: that the members of the wild kingdom, no less than human beings, are an important part of nature's plan for this earth.

Library of Congress Cataloging in Publication Data

Copyright © 1982 by Tara Moore

All rights reserved.

Library of Congress Cataloging in Publication Data

Moore, Tara Hawkins.
  Elephants.

  (The Endangered species)
  Summary: Discusses the world's largest land animal, found only in Africa and Asia, and decreasing in population every year.
  1. Elephants—Juvenile literature. [1. Elephants. 2. Rare animals] I. Title. II. Series.
  QL737.P98M66   1982   599.6'1   82-15656
  ISBN 0-8116-2900-7

Editorial, graphic, and production services under the direction of Cobb/Dunlop, Inc.

Endpaper map, interior and cover designs by Parallelogram/Marsha Cohen

Manufactured in the United States of America.

    Seeing elephants in the wild must surely be one of the most exciting experiences in the world. Elephants are large animals and powerfully built. They are quite majestic wandering through the bush. Their every movement shows a calm self-confidence, their eyes flash a lively intelligence. Armed with camera, sketchbook, and an overwhelming curiosity, I followed the path of the elephants. I have traveled to faraway places such as Kenya and Zambia in Africa and to India and Sri Lanka in Asia to watch, to learn, to know, and to paint these magnificent creatures. *Ah, what a sight to behold!*

Although young elephants (known as calves) are preyed upon by other animals such as lions and leopards in Africa and tigers in Asia, elephants in general have only human beings as an enemy. And yet, in spite of their size, power, intelligence, and lack of natural enemies, the elephant could become an endangered species. That these huge, unforgettable animals are threatened is indeed tragic. The danger to the elephant's existence arises from a very complex set of social and ecological changes. These changes are now taking place within their environment, as we shall discover.

Usually referred to simply as elephants, these animals fall into two distinct groups: the African elephant and the Asiatic elephant. The African elephant is further divided into two sub-groups: one group inhabits the bush country and the other lives in forested regions.

It is a wonderful experience to see an African bush elephant—the world's largest land animal. It stands over 11 feet tall and may weigh as much as 6 tons—about as much as a medium-sized truck. Only certain species of whales exceed the African bush elephant in size. On the other hand, forest elephants are considerably smaller, rarely reaching a height of 8 feet.

Larger than its Asiatic cousin, the African bush elephant has never been domesticated and thus exudes a kind of wild, exciting power. Another real difference between African and Asiatic elephants is probably deeper, more spiritual. The Asiatic elephant seems to have a much calmer nature. Perhaps this is because of their close contact with human beings over many centuries.

 But size and temperment are not the only significant differences between African and Asiatic elephants. There are many noticeable physical differences also. For instance, the African elephant is swaybacked with a sloping forehead and a single dome-shaped formation just above the trunk. On the other hand, the Asiatic elephant is humpbacked and has a bulging forehead that rises into two dome-like formations, one at the front of each temple. Similarly, the African elephant has enormous ears which, when spread, can measure as much as 5 feet across. Its Asiatic relative has rather small, triangular-shaped ears.

Perhaps the most outstanding characteristic of the elephant is its long, flexible trunk. This sensitive limb is made up of thousands of muscles and permits the elephant to perform the important functions of eating, drinking, bathing, communicating, and smelling. Elephants make extensive use of their trunks in rearing their young and in defending themselves. The finger-like 'lips' at the tip of the trunk enable the elephant to grasp such small objects as a single twig, nut, or leaf.

The trunk is so essential to the animal's well-being that whenever there is a danger that might injure it, the elephant will instinctively roll it under so as to protect it from harm.

I once saw a small trunkless calf. Perhaps it had been the victim of a crocodile attack. I stood for a time watching the calf, wondering how it managed to survive. How did it feed itself? Suddenly, as if to calm my fears, the calf knelt on its front knees and scooped up a bunch of grass with its partial trunk. I smiled, amazed at its intelligence and adaptability. The calf would survive in spite of the loss of its trunk.

Elephants have small eyes and poor vision. And in spite of the impressive size of their ears, they have very poor hearing. However, these defects of vision and hearing are compensated for by the sharpness of their other senses. Thus, an elephant's sense of touch and balance are astonishingly well developed—far more than those of human beings. They also have a keen sense of smell. In fact, scientists have found that elephants can easily detect the presence of small quantities of almost odorless substances. This acute sense of smell also provides protection. An elephant, waving its trunk about in the air, can detect the presence of enemies or other dangers that are still a long distance away.

Tusks are very interesting and important to elephants. They are two extremely long incisor teeth that are primarily used as weapons as well as for gathering food. The tusks grow continuously—although they do become worn and may even break off—and are common to both types of African elephant, male and female. However, only the male Asiatic elephant has tusks. Female Asiatic elephants have tushes, long downward curving teeth that are fixed in the gums. Elephant tusks vary considerably, depending on the age and size of the animal. The tusks of the African bush elephant average about 8 or 9 feet and have a combined weight of approximately 250 pounds. Those of Asiatic elephants average 5 to 6 feet in length. Since the tusks are pure, precious ivory, they are in great demand for making jewelry and other art objects. This demand for tusks has led to widespread slaughter of these animals in past years. And even today, illegal hunting for ivory poses a serious problem for the continued existence of these animals.

Today one will frequently see wild elephants without tusks. Thus, while it is apparent that these 'teeth' are important to wild elephants, they seem to be able to adapt to life without them. And yet, I wonder if being robbed of its tusks does not affect an elephant in ways so subtle that humans are unable to understand. For instance, I was once charged by a tuskless female whose suspicious, aggressive nature was probably due to her having been robbed of her tusks.

Elephants are herbivores—plant-eating animals. Their diet consists of all types of grasses, leaves, and fruits. They devour the bark, branches, and the trunks of certain trees, especially that of the acacia and baobab trees. In order to maintain its health and nourish its enormous body, a full-grown African bush elephant may need as much as 300 pounds of food daily. Foraging, searching for food, is the chief activity of these animals. Part of the reason for such an enormous food intake is that elephants chew poorly and have very poor digestive systems. In fact, they digest only about 60 percent of the food they eat.

In order to satisfy its appetite, an elephant may spend up to 18 hours a day feeding. Because of their short thick necks and great height, these animals are unable to bend their heads and take food directly into the mouth. Consequently, every morsel of food that reaches an elephant's stomach gets there by way of the trunk. Thus, an elephant uses its trunk to reach the tender green leaves and shoots at the tops of trees, to pick up fallen fruit, and to uproot large clumps of grass. Moreover, when it is necessary, an elephant will use its trunk in conjunction with its head and tusks to push over a full-grown tree.

In addition to requiring enormous amounts of food, an adult African bush elephant drinks about 30 gallons of water each day. In times of abundant rainfall, the elephants' huge water needs present no problem. But in times of drought, these animals often face severe difficulties. Since droughts occur quite frequently in the African bush country, the herds resort to some rather amazing methods of satisfying their water needs. One of the most common is that of digging wells. These giant animals will search around in a dried-up river bed until they locate a likely spot. They then begin to dig holes, the dry sandlike soil flying up about their legs. At last water bubbles through. The elephants will then stand aside, calmly waiting until the sand has settled and the water is running clear. They then drink in a hierarchy based on age: the older animals first, the calves last. Sufficient water is so essential to the elephants' well-being that in times of extreme drought, they will curl their trunks under and place it deep inside their throats to draw up water that has been taken in earlier.

Acacia and baobab trees are among the elephants' most favorite foods. In a way these animals' love for the leaves of the acacia tree ensures an abundance of these plants. Acacia seeds are more likely to germinate after they have passed through the elephant's digestive system. However, it is quite common to see acres and acres of devastated acacia trees, reduced to broken stumps by herds of foraging elephants. The situation is similar with the baobab tree, the so-called upside-down tree. During droughts, herds of elephants will strip away the bark from baobab trees and then nibble right through the trunks, eating away at the trees' watery, fibrous interior. They will even uproot full-grown trees in order to get at the water-filled roots.

Elephants need large amounts of water not only for drinking but also for maintaining their health in other ways. Because these huge animals do not sweat, they regulate the temperature of their bodies by other means. Thus, in order to keep cool in the hot climate of the bush country, an elephant will continuously fan itself with its ears. They will frequently use their trunks to spray their ears with water so that the fanning will be all the more effective.

Unlike the Asiatic elephant which is known to be a strong and tireless swimmer, the African bush elephant does not seem to like deep water. Nevertheless, they spend a good deal of time wading in large rivers. And, like their Asiatic cousins, they walk the bottom of shallow streams, their flexible trunks held high above the water surface, like a submarine periscope. Aside from providing a means of keeping cool, baths also serve to rid these animals of harmful parasites and annoying insects. Anyone who has experienced the intense tropical heat and varied insect life of the African bush country can well appreciate the value of these long, cool baths.

Water baths are not the only baths elephants take; they often take mud and dust baths, too. Rolling about playfully in shallow ponds and along muddy river banks, they cover their bodies with mud. And frequently they spray themselves with gigantic bursts of dust. These baths are very important in maintaining the elephant's health. Not only does the mud or dust help regulate the animals' body temperature but the baths also protect the elephants' rough but sensitive skin from insects and parasites.

Several years ago in Kenya, I saw a group of some twenty elephants come down to the river to drink and bathe. The water was quite deep and the current swift. The adults waded slowly through the shallows and then moved confidently into the depths, splashing water over themselves as they proceeded. Finally they stopped in the middle of the river, amid the swift current, almost completely submerged in the cool sparkling water. Only their massive heads could be seen.

Suddenly a calf decided to join the adults and ran playfully out into the depths. The calf was immediately caught in the furious current and was in danger of being swept downstream. Helplessly, I stood on the shore, wondering if the calf would be able to make its way back to the shallows. All at once a big female that had been standing peacefully in the middle of the stream moved into the path of the endangered calf. The cow's enormous body provided a solid bulwark for the little animal against the rushing water. Slowly, the other adults gathered around and, working together, they soon managed to get the frightened calf back to safety.

Elephants are nomadic and roam over vast areas in search of sufficient food and water. In recent decades, more and more of the open land and wilderness that was once these animals' natural domain has been taken over by human beings and turned into farms and cattle-grazing areas. This development has led to tragic conflicts between human beings and elephants, since the elephants continue to obey their inborn nomadic instincts. However, in spite of the presence of farms and villages, some elephant herds still gather and follow their old migration routes to new feeding grounds.

Although elephants live in herds of about fifty animals, and may contain as many as one hundred, the small family is the basic social group. Consisting of overlapping generations of females—mothers and daughters—and young males of less than twelve years of age, the elephant family is a completely mother-dominated unit. At about twelve years of age, the males—called bulls—leave the family and go out on their own. Their departure from the unit is usually voluntary. But sometimes a young male may be reluctant to leave and the cows will force him to go. Once a bull leaves the family unit he tends to stay alone, but always within a few miles of a family. Occasionally he may group himself with other bulls for short periods of time.

Wild elephants are completely social and it is very rare to find a solitary one. Those elephants that do break all social ties and lead solitary and peaceful lives are generally males.

Elephant cows bear only one calf at a time. At birth a calf weighs about 250 pounds and stands almost three feet high. Within a year they can feed on vegetation but often they continue to suckle for several more years. Once the calf's tusks began to grow, they become an irritant to the mother, and the calf will then be forced to eat vegetation.

The bulls take no interest in their mates nor in the calves. However, during pregnancy and in the period immediately following birth, the mother and her calf are carefully protected by other females in the family. Although the cow is generally very watchful of her offspring, the task of rearing the young is a matter for the entire family. Sometimes another cow may temporarily "adopt" the calf. She will even allow it to suckle—treating the calf in all respects as though it were her own.

Although elephant calves might appear rather large and robust, they are quite helpless against predators. They need the careful watchfulness and protectiveness of the adults if they are to survive. Fortunately, this protectiveness is ever present, and any predator approaching a calf is asking for trouble.

I once observed a family of elephants being teased by a pack of wild dogs. The adults shook their large heads, spread their ears and began to flap them wildly. As they formed a protective circle around the calves, they bellowed loud, ferocious noises. From time to time a cow would dart out from the circle and scatter the menacing dogs. This cow would then return to the circle and another adult would step forward, trumpet loudly, and charge the pack.

The dogs were making great sport of teasing the elephants when their attention was captured by an approaching rhinoceros and her calf. The elephants, though still angry, relaxed their defensive circle as the wild dogs moved toward the rhino. Like the elephants, the rhino was very protective of her young and the calf stayed close to its mother. The rhino snorted and grunted and charged the wild pack a few times. Finally, the dogs grew tired of trying to separate them and meandered away.

Because elephants are sociable animals, they learn the rules that govern their social structure very early. Each animal seems to know precisely when to assert itself within the family. Consequently, disputes seldom occur. All the cows and calves willingly accept the dominance of the matriarch, the oldest and wisest member of the family. Even among the bulls, fights are rare.

I once saw a herd of 50 or 60 elephants spread over the Nsefu Salt Flats in Zambia. Other animals were grazing peacefully on the broad, open plain—zebras, pukus, impalas, giraffes, and warthogs. The animals had come here to obtain the necessary salts and minerals that supplement their diets. The elephants were divided into several small family groups. Some were eating, others were rolling about in the mud. There were others just standing around, flapping their huge ears. There was no hostility among the elephants or between them and the other animals.

The peaceful nature of the elephant is probably due to the fact that they have no natural enemies in the wild kingdom. They do not establish or defend territory as do some other animals. Rather they roam freely over hundreds of square miles of wilderness, feeding as they go.

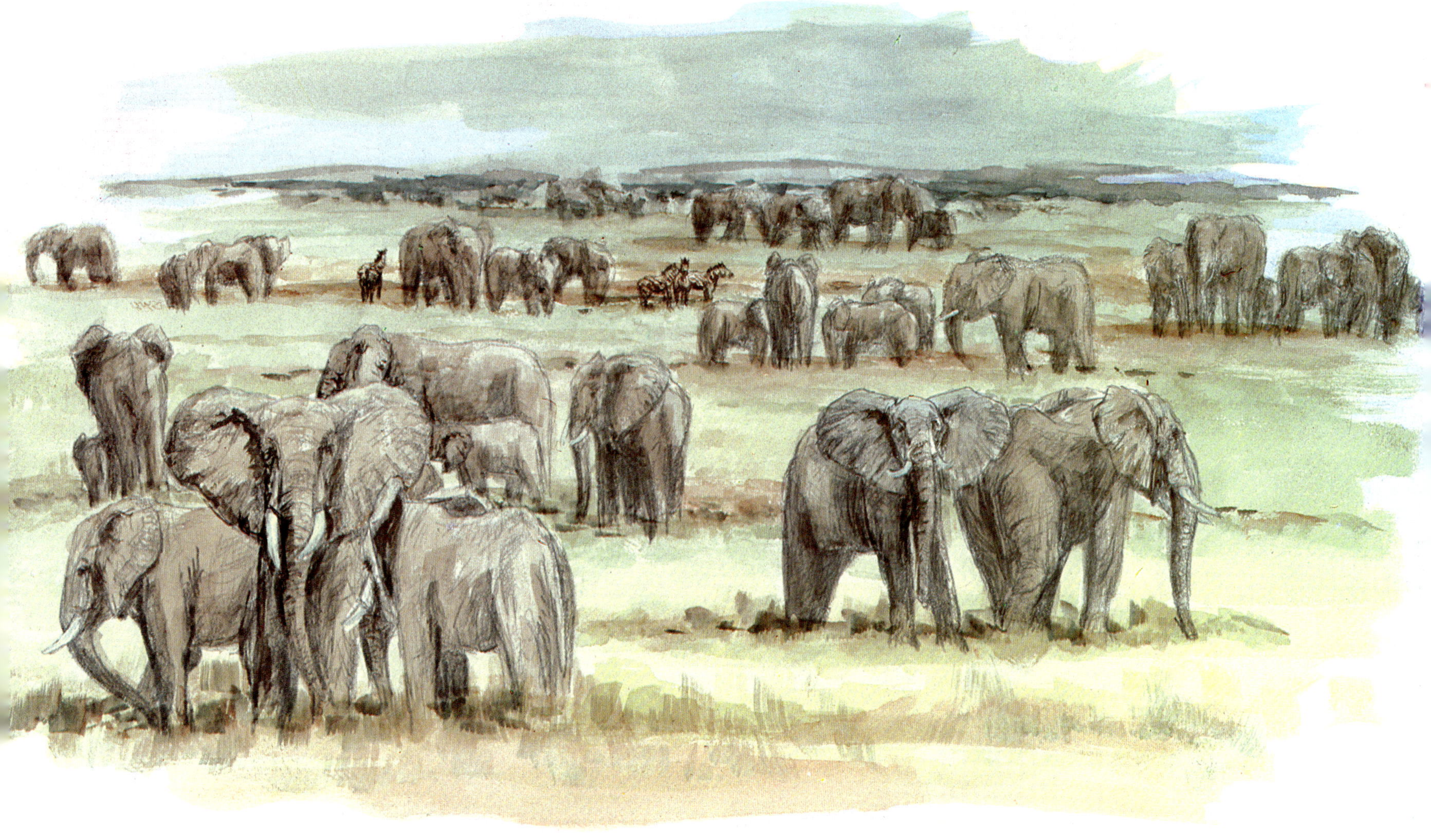

As I watched, a giraffe knelt to drink at one of the waterholes on the salt flats. I was reminded of the little trunkless calf. After all, giraffes kneel to drink, so why not an elephant?

Elephants are highly intelligent animals and display a variety of emotions toward each other. For example, they will aid a wounded or ill family member by supporting it until it has regained strength. In addition to such emotional reactions, these animals make a variety of sounds that are formed into definite voice patterns. Scientists are now convinced that elephants are able to communicate with each other in a very logical and well-developed way.

Touching is one of the most common ways elephants use to communicate with each other. It is almost ceremonial and is used not only among family members but with complete strangers as well. It is wonderful to see them 'speak.'

When the animals approach each other, each heading in a different direction, they raise their trunks. And, as they pass, each briefly and gently touches the tip of its trunk on the forehead of the other and then moves on. Such methods of communication are, to me, another indication of their intelligence.

The close association between human beings and elephants is now more than 5000 years old. Historical records confirm that elephants were used by people long ago in ancient Egypt. This association has lasted down to the present, for human beings and elephants are still found working together in India, Sri Lanka, and other countries of Southeast Asia.

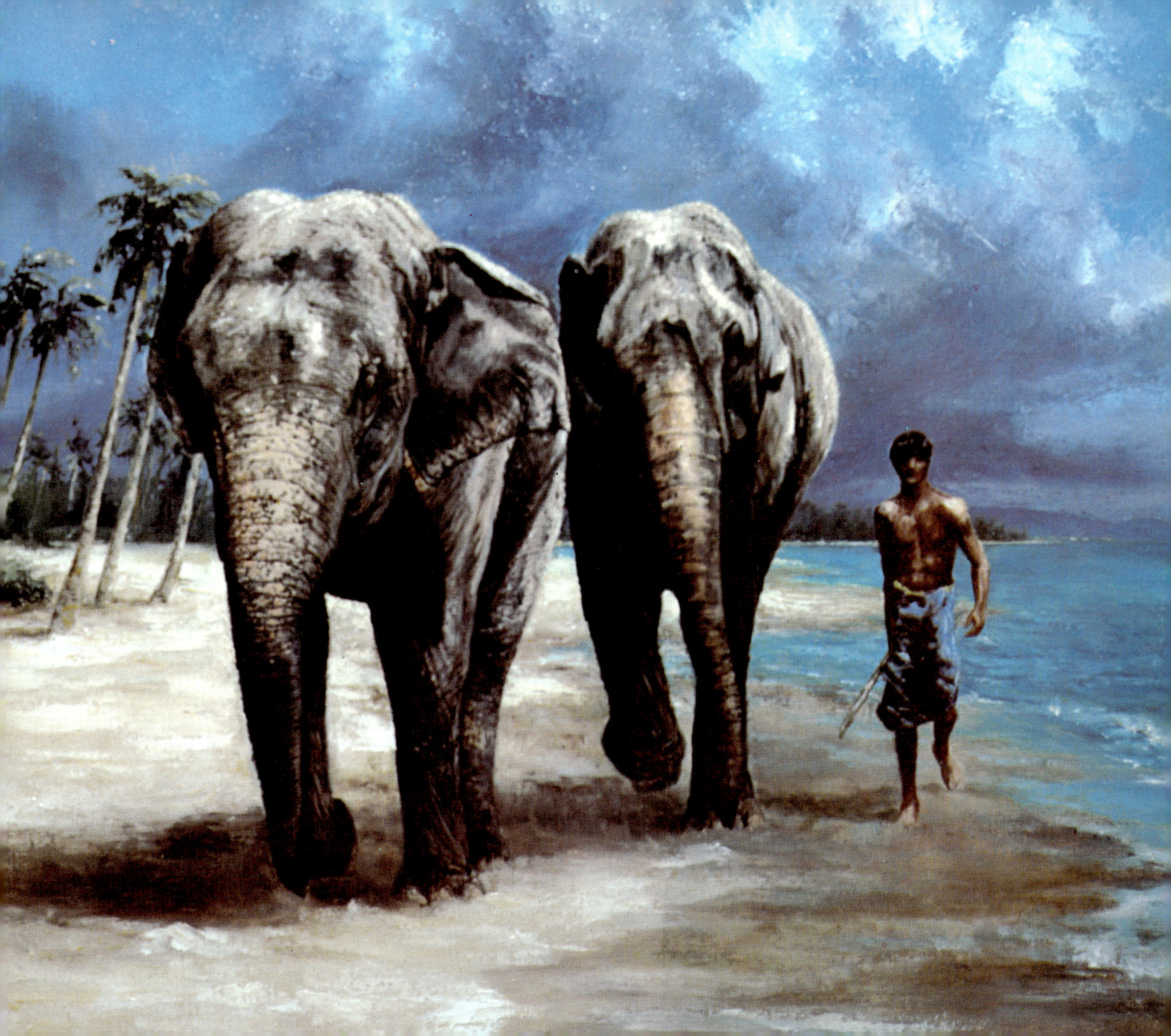

The work elephants used in Southeast Asia are born in the wild. They are captured young, then tamed, and quickly put into training. Females are preferred because they are more docile and alert. Thus, when a cow is about ten years old her training will begin. The *mahout*, the man or boy who trains the elephant generally remains with it for life.

In Southeast Asia, elephants are used for a variety of tasks in heavy labor, entertainment, and parades. They are especially useful in the lumber industry of India and Sri Lanka. Given a few simple commands, they will haul and stack large, heavy logs as well as uproot trees. Elephants are particularly well-suited to such work since they can move through the dense jungles much more easily than tractors, trucks, and bulldozers can. Similarly, in Nepal, they are often the only reliable means of transportation through the thick underbrush and forests.

Elephants also play an important role in the festivals and parades in many Asian countries. And here in the United States, they are circus performers.

The affection which ultimately develops between the mahout and his charge is very deep. The typical relationship between them involves the daily baths which the mahout gives the elephant. The bath consists largely of giving the animal a thorough, careful scrubbing with a coconut shell. During this entire activity the mahout gently talks to her. These baths strengthen the bond of friendship between mahout and elephant, and they also serve the more practical purpose of maintaining the animal's health. For, like their fellows in the wild, these work animals must be kept cool, clean, and free of harmful insects and parasites.

I fully understand the bond of friendship between the mahout and his charge and the value of these refreshing baths. I, too, have bathed an elephant.

Elephants once roamed most of the earth, but today they are found only in certain parts of Africa and Asia. While no exact figures are available for the number of wild elephants, it is certain that their population has steadily decreased over the past 50 years. Countries where wild elephants are found are rapidly modernizing. This requires that more and more of the wilderness be used for towns, farms, villages, and cattle grazing. Fortunately, the governments of these countries have taken some significant steps to preserve the herds. They have passed laws against illegal ivory hunting and have set up wildlife preserves and national forests where these animals can live in peace. Ecologists are not sure whether the elephant herds should be periodically culled (thinned out), or whether nature should be allowed to balance itself in this matter. Are there other solutions for the problem of the existence of these magnificent animals? Perhaps. In the Hindu religion, the god of wisdom is depicted as having the head of an elephant. Maybe wisdom is the key to the elephants' survival. For only by acting wisely can human beings ensure that these giants will not become extinct.

To follow the path of the elephants is a real adventure. The excitement evoked by these wonderful creatures lingers long after I have returned to my studio.